TEACHING WITH AI

A PRACTICAL GUIDE TO NEW ERA OF TEACHING

DR DHEERAJ MEHROTRA

Made with ♥ on the Notion Press Platform
www.notionpress.com

Contents

Preface v

1. Introduction: The AI Revolution In Education 1
2. AI Based Teaching: The Need Of The Hour In India 10
3. Understanding AI In Education 24
4. Implementing AI In The Classroom 36
5. Personalized Learning With AI 46
6. Enhancing Student Engagement Through AI 59
7. AI For Administrative Efficiency 71
8. Ethical Considerations And Challenges 80
9. Future Trends In AI And Education 91
10. Top 25 AI Tools For Educators 102
11. About The Author 111

Books By The Same Author 115

Preface

*Hello and welcome to "**Teaching with AI: A Practical Guide to a New Era of Teaching.**" At a time when the incorporation of Artificial Intelligence (AI) is not only a potential but an essential revolution altering the terrain of instruction and learning, this book comes out at a critical juncture in the development of education. We are on the cusp of a new age as educators, where artificial intelligence (AI) will augment our skills, customize students' learning experiences, and solve old problems in the field.*

Educators enthusiastic about incorporating AI into their lessons will find this book invaluable. Its goal is to illuminate artificial intelligence by providing concrete examples of how these technologies might enhance classroom instruction. This guide will equip new and seasoned educators with the knowledge and skills necessary to succeed in this dynamic field.

The following chapters cover everything from an introduction to artificial intelligence (AI) and its possible uses in the classroom to more in-depth analyses of how to incorporate AI-powered resources into your pedagogical arsenal. We will explore real-life examples and case studies that show how AI has been successfully used in classrooms worldwide. These examples show how AI may help with data analytics, individualized learning, student engagement, and administrative activities.

This book is central to keeping technology in check while allowing human connection. Even while AI provides excellent resources to improve education, no one can ever fully replace a teacher. This guide highlights the need to connect with kids personally, build strong relationships, and support their emotional and social growth. Rather than displacing human teachers, AI should be considered an asset that can supplement human expertise.

As we begin our adventure side by side, I hope you'll welcome the new period with curiosity and a willingness to learn. There are certain obstacles to implementing AI in the classroom, but the potential benefits of making lessons more engaging, accessible, and productive are substantial. If we adopt new technologies with care and ethics, the future of education can be shaped for the better for all students.

I hope this book motivates you to recognize the possibilities of AI in the classroom and provides the tools to make the most of it. Working together can change how people learn, teach, and break new ground in this fascinating field.

Welcome to the dawn of a new age in education.

Best regards,

Dr Dheeraj Mehrotra

Author

www.authordheerajmehrotra.com

Vladimir Vapnik:"The more powerful computers become, the more we can understand the brain. AI is a tool to unlock the secrets of human cognition."

CHAPTER ONE

Introduction: The AI Revolution in Education

Stephen Hawking:"The development of full artificial intelligence could spell the end of the human race."

The introduction of Artificial Intelligence (AI) has ushered in a period of profound revolutionary change across a wide range of industries, and education is at the forefront of this revolution. Traditional educational paradigms are being reshaped by AI technologies, providing unprecedented opportunities to refine teaching practices, tailor learning experiences, and enhance educational outcomes for students worldwide.

The Increasing Role of Artificial Intelligence in Education

The driving forces behind the use of artificial intelligence in educational settings are its adaptability to individual learning demands, the ability to handle massive volumes of data, and the provision of insights that inform tailored instruction. Through the use of adaptive learning platforms and intelligent tutoring systems, artificial intelligence is transforming how educators approach the design of curricula, the evaluation of students, and the management of classrooms.

Educational Platforms That Are Adaptive:

Adaptive learning systems utilize artificial intelligence algorithms to analyze students' learning habits and modify educational content in real time. With this individualized approach, students receive an education that matches their learning methods, strengths, and shortcomings.

(ITS) stands for "intelligent tutoring systems."

Students receive tailored feedback, advice, and support from ITS, which simulates human tutors using artificial intelligence. These methods improve learning efficiency by correcting individuals' misunderstandings and facilitating a deeper comprehension of more complicated theoretical concepts.
With Insights Driven by Data:

Educators can harness data from learning management systems and student interactions with the help of analytics tools driven by artificial intelligence. These insights enable the identification of learning trends, the prediction of student performance, and the optimization of instructional practices to meet educational objectives.

AI's Benefits to the Educational System

Elon Musk:"Artificial intelligence will be the best or worst thing ever for humanity."

Within the realm of education, the implementation of AI presents many appealing advantages:

Artificial intelligence allows creating adaptable and individualized learning experiences, catering to each student's specific requirements, preferences, and learning rate.

Automating administrative activities, including grading and tracking attendance, enables educators to devote more of their attention to the involvement of individual students and the delivery of education, which results in increased efficiency.

AI analytics provides educators with actionable insights that influence evidence-based decision-making, curricular revisions, and targeted interventions to improve student performance. This type of decision-making is referred to as data-driven decision-making.

Considerations and Obstacles to Overcome

Sundar Pichai:"AI is one of the most important things humanity is working on. It is more profound than electricity or fire."

Although the potential advantages of AI in education are substantial, many obstacles need to be overcome:

Ethical Considerations:

Ensuring the ethical use of artificial intelligence is often known as ensuring data privacy, preventing algorithmic prejudice, and providing equal access to AI technologies.

Teacher training provides educators with the information and abilities they need to use artificial intelligence tools in their teaching practices successfully.

The infrastructure and resources initiative addresses gaps in technology infrastructure and access to artificial intelligence technologies across various educational contexts.

What the Future Holds for Artificial Intelligence in Education

When we look into the future, we see that the application of AI in education holds a great deal of promise. Augmented reality (AR) and virtual reality (VR) are innovations that, when paired with adaptive learning systems driven by artificial intelligence, will improve immersive and interactive learning experiences. Furthermore, the ability of artificial intelligence to facilitate worldwide collaboration among educators and students through the transcendence of geographical borders holds the promise of enhancing cross-cultural learning and interaction.

In conclusion, the transformation in education brought about by artificial intelligence constitutes a crucial point in altering the transfer and acquisition of information. When educators make responsible and imaginative use of artificial intelligence technologies, they can open new possibilities for individualized learning, educational justice, and the preparation of students for the difficulties and opportunities that come with living in a digital world that is constantly growing. As we embark on this transformative path, it will be vital for educators, politicians, and technology developers to work together to realize the full potential of artificial intelligence to improve education on a global scale.

Bill Gates:"AI is the ultimate tool that we have to create new tools with. It's going to be the equivalent of the advent of the internet or the PC."

CHAPTER TWO

AI Based Teaching: The Need Of The Hour In India

Teaching Through Artificial Intelligence: India's Educational Revolution

India stands at the threshold of a transformative educational journey, where artificial intelligence becomes the cornerstone of learning. This revolution promises to reshape how millions of children learn, think, and prepare for tomorrow's challenges.

The New Literacy: AI as a Foundational Skill

Transforming Education from the Ground Up

From the academic year 2026-27, artificial intelligence education becomes mandatory from Class 3 onwards across India, marking a historic shift in our educational landscape.

Over 1 crore teachers will be trained for AI teaching under the comprehensive NEP 2020 framework, ensuring quality instruction reaches every corner of the nation.

AI literacy is no longer a supplementary skill—it's an essential competency for India's future workforce, preparing our children for careers that don't yet exist.

India's Bold Curriculum Shift

Primary School Foundation

Interactive AI basics introduce young learners to computational thinking through engaging activities and age-appropriate concepts that spark curiosity.

Middle School Application

Real-world AI applications bridge theory and practice, showing students how AI solves everyday problems in healthcare, agriculture, and transportation.

High School Innovation

Advanced AI innovation projects empower students to create solutions for local challenges, fostering entrepreneurial thinking and technical mastery.

IIT Madras leads the curriculum design, bringing world-class expertise to ensure India's AI education framework meets global standards whilst addressing our unique needs.

The curriculum emphasizes "AI for Public Good", weaving ethics, social responsibility, and critical thinking throughout every lesson, ensuring our students become not just skilled technologists but also conscientious citizens.

Empowering Teachers: From Administrative Burden to Classroom Innovators

Liberation from Routine Tasks

AI tools automate grading, attendance tracking, and record-keeping, freeing teachers to focus on what truly matters—personalized instruction and meaningful student engagement.

Data-Driven Insights

Real-time analytical dashboards highlight individual student learning gaps and strengths, enabling teachers to intervene precisely when and where support is needed most.

Comprehensive Professional Development

Over 10,000 teachers have been trained since 2019 through strategic partnerships with industry leaders like Intel, IBM, and NIELIT, building confidence and competence.

Personalized Learning & Bridging Educational Gaps

Adaptive Intelligence Meets Individual Needs

AI-powered adaptive platforms revolutionize education by tailoring lessons to each student's unique pace and learning style, ensuring no child is left behind or held back.

Multilingual AI tools embrace India's linguistic diversity, providing support in regional languages including Hindi, Tamil, Telugu, and many others—making quality education truly inclusive and accessible.

Assistive AI technologies empower children with disabilities through innovative features like speech-to-text conversion, real-time translation, and customized content delivery, breaking down traditional barriers to learning.

22+	3X	40%
Regional Languages Supported	Faster Learning Progress	Improvement in Engagement
Enabling education in mother tongue	With adaptive AI personalization	Among students with disabilities

Ethical AI Education: Teaching Responsibility Alongside Technical Skills

Preventing Bias & Misinformation

Students learn to identify and address algorithmic bias, recognize misinformation, and understand privacy implications—critical skills for responsible digital citizenship.

Core Ethical Principles

The curriculum integrates AI ethics from early stages, emphasizing fairness, transparency, accountability, and the societal impact of technological decisions.

Global Standards, Local Context

India's approach aligns with UNESCO's global AI ethics framework whilst addressing our unique cultural values, promoting human rights and inclusive development.

> "Teaching AI without ethics is like teaching someone to drive without traffic rules. India is ensuring our children become responsible innovators, not just skilled technologists."

Centre of Excellence in AI for Education

Union Budget Allocation

2025-26 initiative

Fostering Innovation & Research Excellence

A landmark Rs. 500 crore initiative under Union Budget 2025-26 establishes India's Centre of Excellence, driving cutting-edge research and innovation in AI-powered education.

Premier Institutional Collaboration

Strategic partnerships with IITs, NITs, and leading universities develop comprehensive AI modules covering machine learning, robotics, data science, and ethical frameworks.

AI Learning Labs Network

State-of-the-art laboratories established nationwide provide hands-on experiences, enabling students and faculty to experiment with real AI tools and technologies.

Industry Integration

Close collaboration with technology industry leaders ensures curriculum remains relevant, practical, and aligned with evolving workplace requirements and emerging opportunities.

Overcoming Challenges: Infrastructure & the Digital Divide

The Challenge

Rural-urban disparities in internet connectivity and device availability remain significant hurdles, with millions of students lacking consistent access to digital resources.

Government Response

Ambitious programmes like PM eVidya and Digital India aim to bridge these gaps through infrastructure development, device distribution, and connectivity expansion.

Pilot Testing

Innovative pilot projects test AI tools across diverse school environments—from metropolitan schools to remote tribal areas—ensuring solutions work everywhere.

 **Offline AI Solutions:** Recognizing connectivity challenges, developers are creating offline-capable AI learning tools that function without continuous internet access, ensuring uninterrupted education.

Preparing for Viksit Bharat 2047: AI and the Future Workforce

Building Tomorrow's Skilled Workforce Today

Artificial intelligence is expected to create **8 million new jobs by 2030**, fundamentally transforming traditional roles across every sector of India's economy.

Early AI education directly aligns with India's ambitious vision to build a skilled, innovation-driven, future-ready workforce capable of competing globally and driving economic growth.

Strategic upskilling becomes critical not merely to avoid job displacement, but to harness AI's full potential for national development and individual prosperity.

1. **2026-27** — AI education mandatory from Class 3
2. **2030** — 8M new AI-related jobs created
3. **2035** — AI contributes $1 trillion to economy
4. **2047** — Viksit Bharat: Developed India

India Leading the Global AI Education Movement

Comprehensive Strategy

India's holistic approach seamlessly blends cutting-edge technology, robust ethical frameworks, and genuine inclusivity—creating a model admired worldwide.

Massive Scale Impact

Equipping millions of students and teachers to not just survive but truly thrive in an AI-driven world, democratizing access to transformative education.

Global Leadership

Setting a powerful example for nations worldwide, demonstrating how to democratize AI learning whilst building responsible, ethical innovators for tomorrow.

> "India's AI education revolution is not just about teaching technology—it's about empowering a generation to shape the future responsibly, ethically, and inclusively. This is our moment to lead."

Experiential Learning with AI Tools

AI Use by Teachers

Educators leverage AI tools to personalize instruction, assess student performance efficiently, and foster interactive learning environments. These technologies help teachers address diverse classroom needs while focusing on creative and critical thinking skills development.

Experiential Learning with AI Tools

Instant Presentations, Websites, and More with AI | Gamma

Experiential Learning with AI Tools

Experiential Learning with AI Tools

Experiential Learning with AI Tools

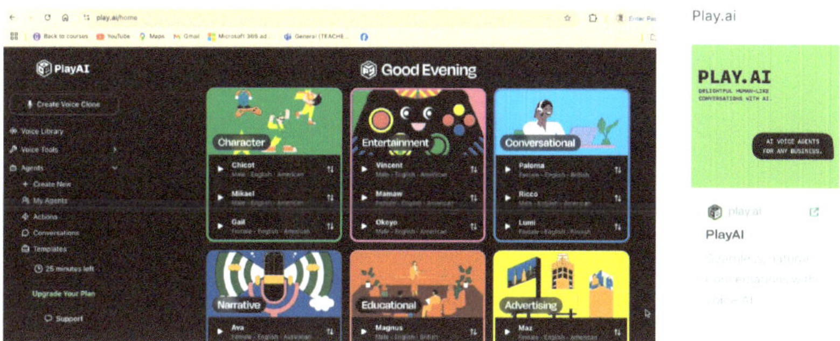

Experiential Learning with AI Tools

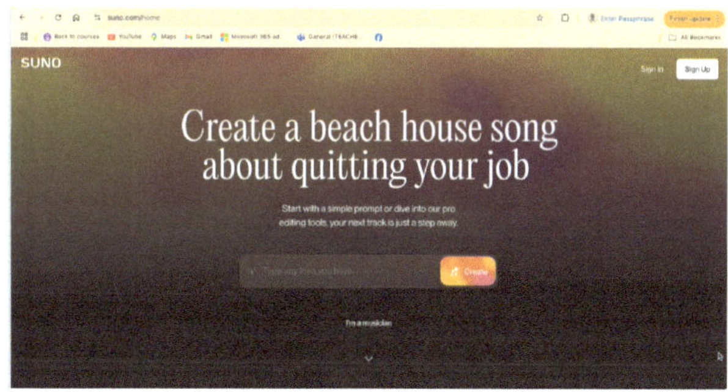

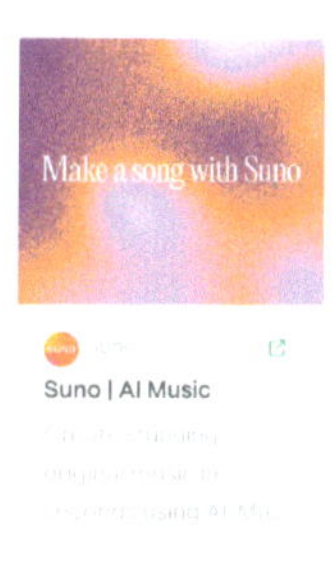

Resources to Accelerate AI Mastery

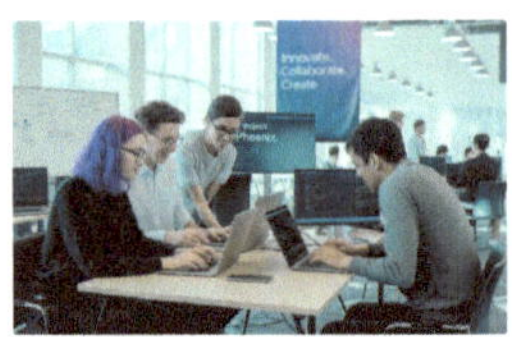

Online Learning

Coursera, edX, and Udacity offering comprehensive AI certificate programmes with industry recognition

Executive Education

University AI centres providing specialized training for mid-career professionals and leaders

Community Engagement

AI practitioner networks and global hackathons offering hands-on experience and valuable connections

Key Takeaways: Your Action Plan

Prioritize Upskilling

Invest in ongoing development of both AI technical knowledge and essential human factors like creativity and judgment

Pursue Cross-functional Projects

Seek opportunities to apply AI in practical contexts across different domains to build versatile fluency

Engage Globally

Connect with international networks and interdisciplinary teams to broaden your perspective and applications

This three-part approach will position you to thrive in the emerging AI-integrated landscape, regardless of your primary discipline or career stage.

Q&A and Further Discussion

Topics for Exploration

- Custom AI learning journeys for your specific discipline or role
- Addressing cross-disciplinary integration challenges in your organization
- Resources tailored to your current skill level and career goals
- Specific questions about the future of AI in your field
- Strategies for effective human-AI collaboration in your work

Conclusion: Mastering AI Skills for the Future

> AI mastery is no longer optional—it's essential for creative, impactful careers across all disciplines.

The cross-disciplinary future of AI is already unfolding. Those who develop interdisciplinary agility and AI fluency will remain relevant and influential as traditional boundaries continue to dissolve. The time to begin this journey is now—through continuous learning, practical application, and collaborative exploration across domains.

CHAPTER THREE

Understanding AI in Education

Andrew Ng:"Artificial intelligence is the new electricity."

Artificial intelligence (AI) is being quickly developed and has substantial educational implications. Educators can use artificial intelligence technologies to improve teaching and learning processes, customize education, expedite administrative operations, and ultimately improve academic outcomes. Understanding the role of artificial intelligence (AI) in education and its potential is essential for educators, administrators, and policymakers who want to educate children for the future.

Understanding AI

Artificial intelligence (AI) refers to the simulation of human intelligence processes by machines, particularly computer systems. Examples of these processes are learning, which is acquiring information and rules for using that information; reasoning, which is employing rules to arrive at approximate or definitive conclusions; and self-correction. Technologies based on AI encompass a wide range of capabilities, such as computer vision, natural language processing, and machine learning.

Learning Machines (ML): Key Artificial Intelligence Technologies in Education

"machine learning" refers to algorithms that allow computers to learn from data and make predictions based on that data. Machine learning can predict future outcomes, monitor student performance, and personalize educational learning experiences.

The acronym "Natural Language Processing" [NLP]

Language processing (NLP) allows computers to comprehend, interpret, and produce human language. In education, examples include chatbots driven by artificial intelligence, virtual assistants, and software for grading written tasks.

Vision on a Computer:

Computer vision allows machines to understand visual input and decide based on that data. In the classroom, it can monitor student participation, automate attendance, and enhance interactive learning resources.

For robotics:

Educational robots can engage students in hands-on learning, particularly those studying STEM disciplines. Furthermore, they can offer individualized support and tutoring services.

The analysis of data:

Data analytics systems powered by artificial intelligence (AI) may process an enormous amount of educational data, providing insights into student performance, identifying trends, and influencing decision-making.

Personalized Learning: Applications of Artificial Intelligence in Education

Artificial intelligence (AI) allows educators to tailor educational content to the specific requirements of individual pupils. Adaptive learning platforms evaluate students' strengths and weaknesses and alter the content to accommodate the findings. This ensures that each student advances at a customized rate.

(ITS) stands for "intelligent tutoring systems."

ITS can deliver one-on-one instruction by simulating human tutors. These systems provide personalized feedback and support and use artificial intelligence to comprehend students' learning methods and challenges.

Grading that is Automated:

AI can automate grading assignments and examinations, particularly for problems requiring short or multiple-choice answers. Tools powered by artificial intelligence can provide feedback on grammar, style, and even content in written tasks.

Conversational agents and virtual assistants:

Chatbots and virtual assistants powered by artificial intelligence can assist students with regular questions, provide immediate feedback, and access resources. These tools can also assist educators by taking care of administrative responsibilities.

The Analytics of Learning:

Ray Kurzweil:"Our technology, our machines, are part of our humanity. We created them to extend ourselves, and that is what it means to be human."

Artificial intelligence can analyze data from various sources, including student information and learning management systems, to provide insights into student engagement and performance. Educators can use this information to identify pupils at risk and adapt interventions.

Creation of Content and Content Curation:

Artificial intelligence can help create and curate instructional content, such as interactive simulations, movies, and quizzes. Additionally, AI can provide students with recommendations for materials pertinent to their learning requirements and preferences.

The inclusiveness and accessibility of:

Artificial intelligence technology can benefit students with disabilities by providing individualized accommodations, such as speech-to-text tools, audio descriptions, and adaptable interfaces.

Advantages of Artificial Intelligence in Education Increased Participation:

Utilizing AI tools that are both interactive and personalized can make the learning process more exciting and enjoyable for students, which can, in turn, boost their motivation and involvement.

Outcomes That Are Better:

Artificial intelligence can facilitate personalized training and timely interventions, improving academic achievements and a more profound comprehension of the subject matter.

Effectiveness: efficiency

Using artificial intelligence, mundane processes such as grading and administrative work can be automated, freeing teachers to concentrate on teaching and supporting students.

With Insights Driven by Data:

Artificial intelligence (AI) offers educators valuable data-driven insights that assist them in making educated decisions on the design of curricula, teaching practices, and student support.

Capacity to Grow:

Artificial intelligence systems may be scaled to accommodate vast numbers of students, making high-quality education available to more pupils.

Considerations and Obstacles to Overcome

John McCarthy:"As soon as it works, no one calls it AI anymore."

Security and Privacy of Information:

The use of artificial intelligence in education creates issues regarding data privacy and security. Protecting student information and ensuring it is handled ethically is paramount.

Both Fairness and Bias:

Artificial intelligence systems can unintentionally reinforce biases in the data they use for training. Therefore, it is vital that applications of artificial intelligence be fair and equitable to prevent current inequities from being exacerbated.

Instruction and Assistance for Teachers:

Instructors need proper training and support for artificial intelligence to be effectively implemented in education. They must acquire the knowledge necessary to utilize AI tools and incorporate them into their instructional activities.

The Infrastructure and the Cost:

It may be challenging to integrate artificial intelligence technology due to the initial expense of these technologies and the requirement for robust infrastructure, particularly in schools with limited resources.

Considerations that are Ethical:

Considering the ethical concerns associated with using artificial intelligence in education is necessary. These concerns include the impact on the relationships between teachers and students and the possibility of becoming overly dependent on technology.

Conclusion:

The application of artificial intelligence has the potential to revolutionize education by enabling tailored learning experiences, enhancing efficiency, and generating insights driven by data. However, to achieve successful integration, it is necessary to overcome difficulties, including data privacy, bias, teacher training, cost, and ethical considerations. Educators and administrators may leverage the power of artificial intelligence to create an educational environment that is more engaging, successful, and inclusive if they thoroughly understand both the possibilities and limitations of AI. Artificial intelligence technology's role in education is anticipated to expand as it continues to develop, providing new chances for innovation and improvement in teaching and learning.

Alan Turing:"We can only see a short distance ahead, but we can see plenty there that needs to be done."

CHAPTER FOUR

Implementing AI in the Classroom

Geoffrey Hinton:"Machines will be capable, within twenty years, of doing any work a man can do."

Artificial intelligence (AI) is revolutionizing many facets of society, and education is no exception. When implemented successfully, AI has the potential to dramatically improve the learning experience through individualized education, automation of administrative activities, and real-time feedback. However, rigorous planning, awareness of ethical issues, and continual support for educators and students are required to achieve successful integration.

Appreciating the Role of AI in Education

Artificial intelligence (AI) in education comprises various technologies and applications to enhance learning and teaching. These include the following:

Systems that modify the level of difficulty and the substance of lessons based on the individual student's performance and the learning style they like are called adaptive learning platforms.

Intelligent Tutoring Systems are tutors powered by artificial intelligence and offer individualized support and feedback.

Computer programs that grade assignments and offer rapid response are known as automated grading tools. These programs allow teachers to devote their attention to more complex duties.

Students have access to support around the clock through chatbots and virtual assistants, which are systems powered by artificial intelligence that handle common inquiries and administrative duties.

Tools that evaluate student data provide insights into learning patterns and results, assisting educators in making decisions guided by the appropriate information.

Taking Measures to Implement Artificial Intelligence in Classroom Evaluation and Planning

Determine Needs and Goals: With the help of artificial intelligence integration, you should determine the individual needs of your students and the goals you set for yourself. One example would be enhancing personalized learning, reducing administrative workload, or improving student engagement.

Analyze the Artificial Intelligence Tools:

Conduct research and analysis on various artificial intelligence (AI) technologies and platforms to identify those most suitable for achieving your objectives. Consider aspects such as cost, compatibility with existing systems, and convenience.

Resources and Infrastructure in the Area

Fei-Fei Li:"The technology itself is not good or evil. It's the way people use it."

Enhance the Technology Infrastructure:

Ensure that your institution's technology infrastructure can support artificial intelligence tools. This process could involve upgrading hardware, improving internet connectivity, and guaranteeing data security.

Make Sure You Have Funding:

Determine potential funding sources for the deployment of artificial intelligence, including grants, partnerships with technology companies, or the reallocation of budgetary resources.

Development of Professional Skills

Provide Educators with Training: Educators and staff should receive extensive training on using artificial intelligence tools effectively. This should involve technical training and pedagogical tactics, and the goal is to incorporate artificial intelligence into the curriculum.

Continuous Assistance:

Establish a support system for educators, including opportunities for continuous professional development and access to technological assistance.

Matters with Ethical Implications

Implement stringent procedures to protect student data and maintain compliance with requirements such as the General Data Protection Regulation (GDPR) and the Family Educational Rights and Privacy Act (FERPA). All parties involved must comprehend the significance of maintaining data privacy and security.

Both Fairness and Bias:

Ensure that artificial intelligence systems are subjected to regular audits to check for biases and treat all students fairly and equally.

Pilot Programs and Audience Responses

An excellent place to start is with a pilot program to evaluate artificial intelligence tools in a controlled setting. This allows you to discover problems and collect feedback before implementing the solution on a larger scale.

Gain Input from Others:

It is essential to routinely collect input from students, teachers, and other potential stakeholders to evaluate the efficiency of AI tools and make any necessary improvements.

Continuous Monitoring and Implementation on a Large Scale

Implementing AI Tools Once the pilot program has been approved, the next step is implementing AI tools throughout the school or district. For this shift, all educators must receive proper preparation and support.

Evaluate and Monitor:

It is essential to continuously evaluate and monitor AI's influence on learning and teaching. Data analytics allows for evaluating results and making well-informed judgments about additional adjustments or enhancements.

The Advantages of Using AI in the Classroom

Personalized Learning: Artificial intelligence can create learning experiences that are customized to meet the specific requirements of each learner, enhancing engagement and outcomes.

Efficiency:

Artificial intelligence systems can automate mundane chores such as grading and tracking attendance, enabling teachers to devote more attention to teaching and interacting with students.

Artificial intelligence (AI) to provide quick feedback on assignments and exams enables students to comprehend their progress better and identify areas in which they may increase their performance.

Interactive artificial intelligence (AI) solutions, such as virtual reality (VR) and gamified learning platforms, have the potential to make learning more exciting and pleasurable for students.

Data-driven insights: Analytics powered by artificial intelligence offer useful insights into students' performance and learning patterns, thereby assisting instructors in making informed decisions.

Considerations and Obstacles to Overcome

Eliminate the digital divide by ensuring all students have access to the technology they need to use artificial intelligence tools. Acting to close the digital divide is necessary to stop the spread of educational inequality.

Preparedness of Teachers:

Not all teachers may be comfortable using AI tools. Sufficient training and assistance are necessary to guarantee a successful implementation.

Artificial intelligence (AI) technologies and infrastructure may require a considerable initial investment. The costs must be carefully considered, and the various funding possibilities must be investigated.

Concerns Regarding Ethics

Addressing ethical concerns regarding data privacy, security, and bias is vital to retaining trust and justice in applying artificial intelligence.

Conclusion:

The use of artificial intelligence in the classroom can significantly improve education by delivering individualized educational experiences, enhancing operational efficiency, and providing feedback in real-time, among other benefits. Nevertheless, to achieve successful integration, careful planning, consideration of ethical issues, and ongoing support for both educators and students are necessary.

Educational institutions can harness the power of artificial intelligence to produce a more dynamic, engaging, and effective learning environment if they take a careful and strategic approach.

Steve Jobs:"I think that the biggest innovations of the 21st century will be at the intersection of biology and technology. A new era is beginning."

CHAPTER FIVE

Personalized Learning with AI

Mark Zuckerberg:"The real question is, when will we draft an artificial intelligence bill of rights? What will that consist of? And who will get to decide that?"

Personalized learning refers to customizing educational experiences to cater to each learner's specific requirements, preferences, and capabilities. Artificial intelligence technology plays a significant role in making this vision a reality by providing tools and systems that can adjust in real-time to each individual's unique learning patterns. Using artificial intelligence, instructors can deliver individualized instruction, boost student engagement, and improve educational outcomes.

The Function of Artificial Intelligence in the Process of Personalized Learning
Through several vital mechanisms, artificial intelligence technology has the potential to transform traditional education into a more individualized and student-centred experience.

Educational Platforms That Are Adaptive:

Adaptive learning platforms use artificial intelligence to evaluate students' performance and dynamically modify the difficulty level and the specific information provided. These platforms allow for creating individualized routes, guaranteeing that students will receive education and practice at the appropriate difficulty level. Some of them stand as follows:

Quizizz

With Quizizz, teachers can design quizzes that will create a personalized learning path based on each student's responses.

Teachers can also create lessons with Quizizz, which now has an AI enhancement that can adjust question difficulty, check grammar, and redesign questions to reflect real-world scenarios, with more features on the way.

https://quizizz.com/?lng=en

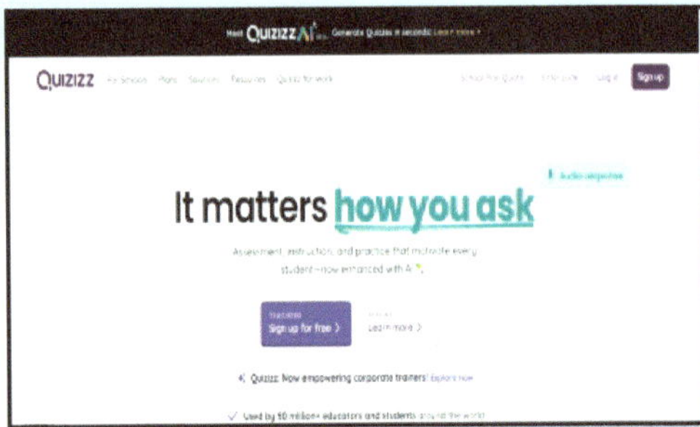

Slidesgo

For creative presentation!

This tool provides access to free templates via Google Slides and now has the AI Presentation Maker. With this new functionality, presentations can be created within minutes. Simply choose a topic; select a tone such as casual, creative, or professional; make changes; and download your presentation. A time-saver for sure!

https://slidesgo.com/

https://www.presentations.ai/

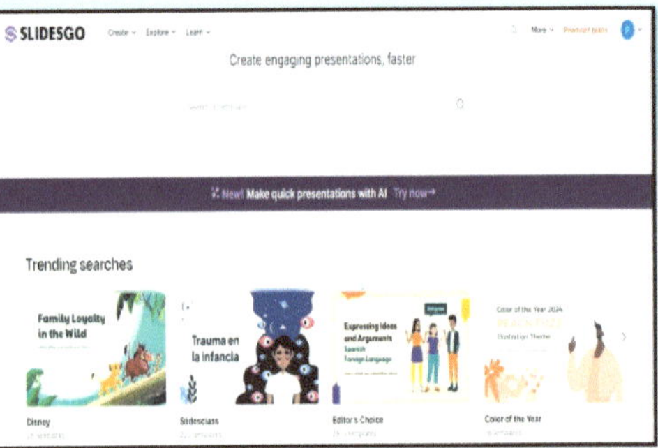

Textfx

For creative writing!

TextFX is an AI experiment that uses Google's PaLM 2 large language model. It is a collection of 10 tools by google!

These 10 tools are designed to expand the writing process by generating creative possibilities with text and language.

https://textfx.withgoogle.com/

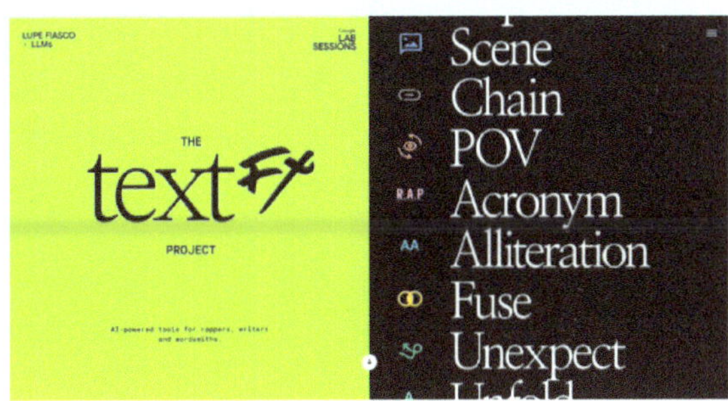

Polite Post

Rewriting your emails with AI to be professional

Very simple to use tool!

Use AI to fix your email to make it professional and work safe!

https://politepost.net/

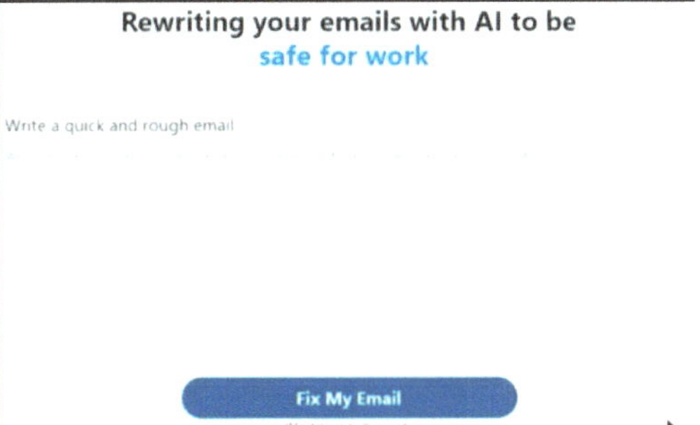

Eduaide

Creating lesson plans with AI to be professional

- Lesson plan **Instructional Planning Without Boundaries.**
- Spend more time on your students, less on administrative tasks and cobbling together resources, with Eduaide.Ai's lesson planning platform.

https://www.eduaide.ai/app/generator

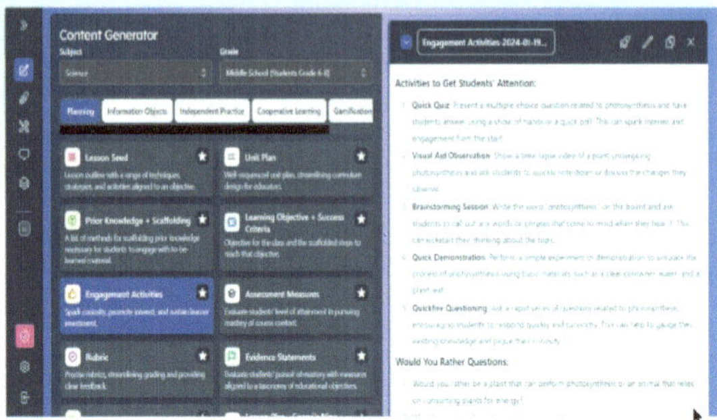

Curipod

Creating lesson plans with AI to be professional

This website enables teachers to create interactive lessons in minutes using AI. Students can explore various topics, and the AI functionality helps generate customized lessons tailored to their learning needs.

Teachers simply type in a topic, and a ready-to-run lesson is generated with text, images, and activities such as polls, open-ended responses, word clouds, and more.

https://curipod.com

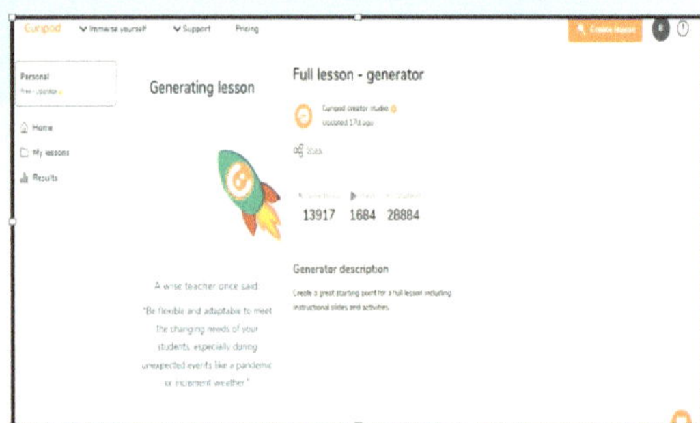

(ITS) stands for "intelligent tutoring systems."

ITS uses artificial intelligence to replicate one-on-one

tutoring by adjusting to the specific educational requirements of individual students. By providing students with tailored tips, feedback, and explanations, these systems assist students in comprehending complex subjects and maintaining their interest.

Predictive modelling and learning analytics will be discussed.

Learning analytics powered by artificial intelligence monitor and analyze various data points, including quiz scores, assignment completion rates, and interaction patterns. Predictive models can identify students at risk of falling behind in their studies and recommend tailored interventions.

The acronym "Natural Language Processing" [NLP]

NLP allows artificial intelligence systems to comprehend and respond to student input in natural language. This technology can be utilized in chatbots, virtual assistants, and interactive educational content to provide individualized assistance and improve the overall quality of the educational experience.

Personalized Learning Driven by Artificial Intelligence: Key Components
The Profiling of Students:

Artificial intelligence systems generate comprehensive profiles for each student using information gathered about a student's learning patterns, interests, talents, and limitations. These profiles allow the learning experience to be tailored to fit the specific requirements of each individual. A Personalization of the Content:

The learning content is personalized by artificial intelligence based on the student's profile.

For example, it can suggest particular videos, articles, activities, or even complete learning modules that are according to the student's preferred learning method and current level of comprehension.

Continuous and Real-Time Evaluation and Feedback:

Giving students real-time performance feedback makes learning more accessible. This enables them to comprehend their errors rapidly and improve. Continuous evaluation is beneficial in determining where there are learning gaps and resolving them as soon as possible.

Differentiated Learning Pathways:

Artificial intelligence can help create a flexible learning route that can be altered based on the learner's development and changing needs. Thanks to this flexibility arrangement, students will not become bored with repeated material or overwhelmed by too-difficult content.

Improving Engagement Through Personalized Learning with Artificial Intelligence Benefits:

Presenting pertinent and sufficiently challenging material through personalized content and adaptive learning experiences sustains students' engagement.

Outcomes of Learning That Are Improved:

When training is tailored to students' particular requirements, students can comprehend concepts more thoroughly and remember knowledge for longer, leading to improved academic performance.

A Higher Level of Motivation:

Students are more likely to be motivated and to take an active role in their education when the learning experiences they participate in are linked with their interests and characteristics that they already possess.

Support for a Wide Range of Educational Requirements:

Students with various learning needs, including those with disabilities, can benefit from personalized learning driven by artificial intelligence (AI), which offers individualized accommodations and learning tools.

Considerations and Obstacles to Overcome

Even though artificial intelligence presents a significant opportunity for individualized education, several obstacles and factors need to be taken into consideration:

Security and Privacy of Information:

Collecting and using student data poses significant privacy and security risks. Therefore, it is of the utmost importance to implement stringent data protection measures and ensure transparency regarding data use.

AI Algorithms That Are Biased:

Artificial intelligence (AI) systems can unintentionally reinforce biases already in their training data, resulting in unjust treatment of particular student groups. To reduce the impact of bias, ongoing monitoring and refinement of algorithms are necessary.

A Fair and Equal Access:

It is essential to ensure all students can access tailored learning tools powered by artificial intelligence. Among these efforts are efforts to close the digital gap and provide essential services to underserved communities.

Instruction and Assistance for Teachers:

Teachers require sufficient training and assistance to incorporate artificial intelligence tools into their instructional practices successfully. The technical features of artificial intelligence (AI) and its instructional consequences should be the primary emphasis of professional development programs.

Towards the Future Paths

Exciting opportunities lie ahead for tailored learning with artificial intelligence in the future. To name a few examples of forthcoming innovations:

Advanced Artificial Intelligence Models:

Continuing breakthroughs in artificial intelligence, such as deep learning and reinforcement learning, will improve the capabilities of personalized learning systems, making them superior in accuracy and efficiency.

Combining Our Technologies with Those of Others:

The integration of artificial intelligence (AI) with other developing technologies, such as augmented reality (AR) and virtual reality (VR), has the potential to generate immersive and interactive learning experiences and further personalize education.

Learning That Lasts a Lifetime:

As a means of assisting individuals in continuously acquiring new skills and knowledge, personalized learning powered by artificial intelligence has the potential to go beyond the scope of traditional schooling and promote lifetime learning and professional growth.

Collaboration Across the Ages:

Artificial intelligence has the potential to enhance global collaboration by connecting students and teachers from different regions of the world. This can be accomplished by providing cross-cultural learning experiences and sharing best practices.

Nick Bostrom:"Machine intelligence is the last invention that humanity will ever need to make."

Conclusion:

Artificial intelligence has the potential to revolutionize personalized learning by delivering educational experiences that are individualized, adaptable, and entertaining and that are tuned to the specific requirements of each learner. By utilizing artificial intelligence, instructors can improve learning outcomes, increase student engagement, and cater to various learning requirements. On the other hand, to fully enjoy the benefits of AI-driven personalized learning, it is vital to overcome data protection, prejudice, equitable access, and teacher training difficulties. With the ongoing development of technology, the opportunities to create learning environments that are more efficient and welcoming to all students will increase, thereby opening the way for a new age in the field of education.

CHAPTER SIX

Enhancing Student Engagement through AI

Ginni Rometty:"Some people call this artificial intelligence, but the reality is this technology will enhance us. So instead of artificial intelligence, I think we'll augment our intelligence."

The degree to which students are engaged in the learning process is an essential component that directly impacts their motivation, retention, and academic accomplishment. This is accomplished through individualized learning experiences, interactive information, and real-time feedback, all made possible by artificial intelligence (AI), which offers revolutionary tools and tactics. By utilizing AI, educators can build a learning environment that is both dynamic and immersive, and that responds to students' varied requirements.

Customized Educational Experiences for Students

Using artificial intelligence, educational content and activities may be adapted to fit each student's specific requirements and preferences, resulting in a more engaging and productive learning experience.

Learning Systems That Are Adaptive:

Adaptive learning systems, powered by artificial intelligence, modify the difficulty level and the type of content based on a student's performance and learning style. These systems continuously analyze student data to deliver individualized recommendations. This ensures that students are challenged appropriately and can move throughout the course at their own pace.

Learner-tailored education programs:

When AI is used to design individualized learning routes for students, it can consider their interests, talents, and career aspirations. Artificial intelligence helps maintain students' interest and motivation to learn by providing relevant and meaningful knowledge.

Systems that are Intelligent in Tutoring:

Intelligent tutoring systems powered by artificial

intelligence offer one-on-one assistance, simulating the course of contact with a human tutor. These systems provide students with individualized explanations, tips, and feedback, which assists them in comprehending complex concepts and maintaining their interest in the subject matter.

Learning that is both interactive and immersive.

Artificial intelligence makes it possible to create learning experiences that are both interactive and immersive, thereby capturing students‘ attention and encouraging them to participate actively.

Pedro Domingos:"Algorithms are not arbiters of objective truth and fairness. They can easily reinforce human prejudices."

Augmented Reality (AR) and Virtual Reality (VR) are the terms.

Artificial intelligence can improve virtual and augmented reality experiences by creating realistic and interactive virtual worlds. Using these tools, students can investigate historical events, carry out scientific experiments, or practice skills that are applicable in the real world safely and entertainingly.

The use of games:

Artificial intelligence can include gamification components in educational content, such as points, badges, and leaderboards. These components make learning more enjoyable and competitive, encouraging students to remain engaged and motivated.

Interactive simulations:

Students have the opportunity to experiment and investigate many concepts inside a supervised and virtual setting through the use of simulations powered by artificial intelligence (AI). The adaptability of these simulations allows them to respond to the learner's activities, thereby delivering instant feedback and increasing engagement.

Provision of Real-Time Feedback and Evaluation

The ability of artificial intelligence to deliver feedback and assessment in real time enables pupils to comprehend their progress immediately and identify areas for improvement.

Feedback that is Automated:

AI systems can analyze students' responses and provide immediate and detailed feedback. This quick feedback helps students fix their mistakes and gain a deeper understanding of subjects, keeping them involved in learning.

Formative evaluations include:

Formative assessments can be made more accessible with artificial intelligence by continuously evaluating student performance and determining the areas in which students require further assistance. This continual evaluation helps to keep students on track and engaged with the curriculum, which helps to achieve this goal.

Keeping Tabs on Progress:

AI systems can monitor students‘ progress, providing insights into their educational path. Using this information, instructors can customize education and support to maintain students' interest and motivation.

Demis Hassabis:"AI is about figuring out how to make machines that can learn and adapt like humans."

Learning Through Collaboration

Artificial intelligence can improve collaborative learning by connecting students and promoting communication and interaction.

AI-Powered Platforms for Collaborative Workouts:

Artificial intelligence can support collaboration platforms that allow students to work together on projects and assignments. To facilitate productive collaboration, these platforms can make recommendations on pertinent resources, supply communication tools, and monitor the dynamics of the group.

Both mentoring and tutoring by peers:

Artificial intelligence can pair pupils with peers or mentors who can provide support and guidance. By enabling students to tutor and mentor one another, artificial intelligence contributes to developing a collaborative learning environment that encourages participation and mutual assistance.

Internet-Based Classrooms:

Artificial intelligence can improve virtual classrooms by providing real-time engagement and collaboration tools. Features such as live polls, breakout rooms, and virtual whiteboards can create an interactive and exciting online learning experience.

Motivating and providing emotional support

Additionally, AI has the potential to comprehend and cater to students' emotional and motivational needs.

The analysis of sentiment:

Artificial intelligence can determine students' emotional states and interest levels using both written and spoken language. Because of this information, instructors can provide timely assistance and interventions to maintain pupils' motivation.

Messages of Hope and Inspiration Tailored to You:

Students can receive individualized reminders and motivating messages from artificial intelligence, encouraging them to remain on track with their studies and engaged with them. The learner's performance and preferences might be considered when customizing these messages.

Bots that provide emotional support:

Students can safely communicate their feelings and worries through emotional support bots driven by artificial intelligence. If necessary, these bots can provide guidance, resources, and recommendations to human counsellors to assist in overcoming emotional barriers to involvement.

Conclusion

Through the provision of individualized learning experiences, interactive information, real-time feedback, and emotional support, artificial intelligence (AI) provides powerful tools that can assist in increasing student engagement. By utilizing artificial intelligence, educators can build a learning environment that is both dynamic and immersive, and that responds to the varied requirements of students. As artificial intelligence (AI) advances, its potential to revolutionize education and enhance student engagement will only increase. This will pave the way for learning experiences that are more efficient and relevant to all students. It is vital to address ethical considerations, assure equal access, and provide ongoing training and support for educators and students in using artificial intelligence technology to achieve these benefits fully.

Isaac Asimov:"I do not fear computers. I fear the lack of them."

CHAPTER SEVEN

AI FOR ADMINISTRATIVE EFFICIENCY

Arthur C. Clarke:"Any sufficiently advanced technology is indistinguishable from magic."

The education industry is no exception to the transformation that artificial intelligence (AI) brings in various fields. One of the most significant effects that AI can have on education is the possibility that it will improve administrative efficiency. AI has the potential to liberate critical time and resources by automating mundane processes, optimizing resource allocation, and offering insightful data analytics. This liberation will enable educators to devote more attention to teaching and less to paperwork.

Tasks that are routinely performed

Through automation, artificial intelligence has the potential to lessen the load of ordinary administrative duties drastically. This helps reduce wasted time and guarantees that administrative procedures are carried out with greater precision and uniformity.

Evaluation and marking of grades:

Assignment and examination grading can be automated by systems driven by artificial intelligence, which will provide students with fast feedback. These systems evaluate written responses through the utilization of natural language processing (NLP) and machine learning techniques, which guarantee consistency and objectivity. Automated grading frees up time for teachers, enabling them to concentrate on more difficult duties that require some degree of human judgment.

Administration of Attendance:

Artificial intelligence systems can automate tracking attendance using facial recognition technology or intelligent ID card systems. These systems can precisely record student attendance in real-time, reducing the amount of administrative work teachers have to do and ensuring that attendance records are accurate.

Making Plans and Organizing Timetables:

Artificial intelligence has the potential to improve class, test, and event scheduling by examining various parameters, including room availability, teacher schedules, and student preferences. This would minimize the likelihood of scheduling conflicts and make the most of available resources.

Systems that automate communication:

Chatbots and virtual assistants powered by artificial intelligence can address common questions from staff, parents, and students. These systems can provide fast solutions to frequently asked queries, arrange appointments, and send reminders, streamlining the communication processes.

Administration and Examination of Data

These valuable insights can enhance decision-making and increase administrative efficiency. Artificial intelligence's ability to process and analyze vast volumes of data delivers these insights.

Analytics of the Performance of Students:

Artificial intelligence systems can analyze data on student performance to detect patterns, strengths, and areas that require work. This information allows instructors to tailor their instructional tactics better to better meet their pupils' needs. In addition, predictive analytics can identify kids who are in danger of falling behind, enabling early intervention to be implemented accordingly.

A Distribution of Resources:

By studying consumption patterns and projecting future requirements, artificial intelligence can potentially improve the distribution of resources such as textbooks, equipment, and facilities. In this way, resources are utilized effectively and are made available at the precise moment they are required.

Handling of Financial Matters:

Artificial intelligence has the potential to simplify certain aspects of financial administration, such as budgeting, payroll, and spending tracking. Automated financial systems can help improve the efficiency of financial planning and management by lowering the number of errors that occur, increasing transparency, and providing real-time insights into the financial system's state.

Facilitating Better Decision-Making

Using artificial intelligence, school administrators can gain insights driven by data, improving decision-making processes and ultimately resulting in better outcomes for children and staff.

The Planning of Strategies:

Artificial intelligence analytics can be very helpful for strategic planning by providing insights into enrollment trends, demographic fluctuations, and academic achievement. Access to this information enables school administrators to make educated decisions regarding curricula development, staffing, and resource distribution.

Establishment of Policies:

Artificial intelligence can evaluate the consequences of existing policies and forecast the possible outcomes of future policies. This strategy, which is driven by data, guarantees that the school's policies are efficient and in line with the institution's goals and objectives.

Management of Emergencies:

Artificial intelligence systems can assist crisis management by delivering real-time data and predictive analytics. In a public health emergency, artificial intelligence can monitor the spread of illness throughout the school community, thereby assisting administrators in making prompt decisions to safeguard children and staff.

Enhancing Capacity for Operational Efficiency

Artificial intelligence has the potential to dramatically increase educational institutions' overall operational efficiency by effectively automating and optimizing various administrative chores.

In addition to Facility Management and Maintenance:

Systems powered by artificial intelligence can monitor the status of school infrastructure and anticipate the need for maintenance. This preventative strategy cuts down on facility downtime and guarantees that the facilities are always in good shape, thereby offering a secure and conducive learning environment.

Management of Transportation:

Artificial intelligence can improve school transportation by monitoring traffic patterns, student addresses, and bus routes. Consequently, it guarantees effective and punctual transportation, lowering expenses and minimizing environmental impact.

Management of the Inventory:

AI systems can manage inventories by monitoring the utilization of goods and equipment and their availability. This helps guarantee that schools always have the required materials, which reduces waste and improves resource management.

Conclusion

A significant amount of potential exists for artificial intelligence to improve administrative efficiency in educational institutions. By automating mundane chores, giving valuable data insights, and optimizing resource allocation, artificial intelligence enables educators and administrators to concentrate on their primary job: providing students with an education of the highest possible quality. Implementing artificial intelligence in administrative functions not only enhances operational efficiency but also results in an educational setting that is more flexible, adaptable, and focused on the needs of students. Schools must continue implementing AI technologies to guarantee that the benefits of artificial intelligence in education are maximized. It is also essential that ethical considerations be addressed, that data privacy be protected, and that staff receive continual training and support.

Eliezer Yudkowsky:"By far the greatest danger of Artificial Intelligence is that people conclude too early that they understand it."

CHAPTER EIGHT

Ethical Considerations and Challenges

Eric Schmidt:"The rise of powerful AI will be either the best or the worst thing ever to happen to humanity. We do not yet know which."

We must address the ethical considerations and challenges accompanying the incorporation of artificial intelligence (AI) in education as we take advantage of AI's promise. Even though synthetic intelligence can dramatically improve education and learning, it also raises concerns that educators, politicians, and technologists must carefully navigate.

Security and Privacy of Information

Regarding artificial intelligence in education, one of the most significant ethical problems is protecting student data and privacy. Artificial intelligence systems frequently require enormous volumes of data to work well, which raises the following issues:

Student Information Protection and Security:

Artificial intelligence technology systems gather and analyze extensive student data, including academic performance, personal characteristics, and behavioural tendencies. Protecting this data from being compromised or accessed by unauthorized parties is paramount. Institutions must deploy highly effective encryption and cybersecurity procedures to protect sensitive information.

Control of Data and Obtaining Consent:

Students and their guardians must clearly understand who owns their data. Educational institutions are required to get the students' express agreement before collecting and using student information. Policies should be open and honest about the data being gathered, how it will be utilized, and who will have access to it.

Observance of all regulations:

Educational institutions must comply with regulations such as the General Data Protection Regulation (GDPR) in Europe and the Family Educational Rights and Privacy Act

(FERPA) in the United States to maintain compliance with data protection laws. These regulations govern the administration of data and preserve the confidentiality of student information.

Access and Fairness in Distribution

The application of artificial intelligence in education has the promise of individualized learning and improved outcomes; yet, if it is not implemented wisely, it also has the potential to worsen existing inequities:

To bridge the digital divide:

Students need a dependable internet connection and current gadgets to access instructional resources powered by artificial intelligence. This may not be available to all students, particularly those who live in rural or economically disadvantaged locations. To prevent the educational gap from growing even further, efforts must be made to guarantee everyone equal access to technology.

Both Fairness and Bias:

Artificial intelligence (AI) systems can unintentionally reinforce biases already present in their training data, resulting in unjust treatment of particular student groups. To reduce the effects of bias, it is necessary to create and deploy algorithms that are open to scrutiny and designed to eliminate bias. Monitoring and updating AI systems continuously can ensure that they are applied fairly.

Regarding Accessibility and Inclusivity:

Artificial intelligence products should be created to be accessible and inclusive to all pupils, including those with disabilities. As part of this process, user-friendly interfaces must be developed, many languages must be supported, and allowances must be made for various educational requirements.

Douglas Hofstadter:"I think it's very important to have a feedback loop, where you're constantly thinking about what you've done and how you could be doing it better."

Repercussions for the Instructional Profession

The incorporation of artificial intelligence into educational settings raises significant concerns regarding the function of educators and the nature of their work:

In the realm of professional judgment and teacher autonomy:

Although AI systems have the potential to offer instructors vital support, they should not be allowed to compromise teachers' professional judgment or autonomy. Educators must maintain the ability to make decisions based on their knowledge and comprehension of their students' requirements.

Instruction & Continuing Education for Professionals:

As artificial intelligence (AI) in education grows more widespread, educators must participate in continual professional development to acquire the knowledge and abilities necessary to use AI tools effectively. The technical features of artificial intelligence (AI) and the pedagogical consequences of its application should be the primary emphasis of training programs.

Displacement of Workers and Transformation of Work:

There is a worrying possibility that artificial intelligence will result in the loss of jobs in the education industry. On the other hand, artificial intelligence ought to be regarded as a tool that can supplement rather than replace the function of educators. By taking over administrative responsibilities and offering individualized support, artificial intelligence can enable teachers to devote more attention to teaching and student involvement.

Rodney Brooks:"The biggest challenge for artificial intelligence is understanding intelligence itself."

Use of Artificial Intelligence Technologies in an Ethical Manner

Several important factors need to be taken into consideration to guarantee the ethical application of artificial intelligence in educational settings:

A commitment to openness and responsibility:

Artificial intelligence systems ought to function transparently, with detailed explanations of the decision-making process. Institutions must take responsibility for the results of their implementations of artificial intelligence and provide channels to rectify any problems that may arise.
Observation and Intervention by Human Beings:

Artificial intelligence systems should supplement human control rather than replace it. When necessary, educators and administrators should be able to intervene and overrule judgments made by artificial intelligence to guarantee the greatest possible outcomes for children.

Creating Standard Operating Procedures and Ethical Guidelines:

The development and application of artificial intelligence in educational settings require the establishment of ethical principles and standards. To ensure that these standards satisfy the educational community's many requirements and concerns, they should be developed with educators, technologists, policymakers, and other stakeholders.

As a part of the conclusion, the application of artificial intelligence (AI) in educational settings presents enormous prospects for improving teaching and learning. On the other hand, it also raises substantial ethical concerns and issues that must be addressed to guarantee that artificial intelligence will benefit all students ethically and equitably. We can negotiate these hurdles and make the most of the potential that artificial intelligence has to offer in the field of education if we place a high priority on data privacy and security, promote diversity and access, provide support for the teaching profession, and ensure that AI technologies are used ethically. Taking this approach, which is intelligent and responsible, will assist in establishing a future in which artificial intelligence contributes to an educational landscape that is more inclusive, effective, and dynamic.

Gary Kasparov:"Machines will never be as intelligent as humans, but they can be useful tools to help us become more intelligent ourselves."

CHAPTER NINE

Future Trends in AI and Education

Kevin Kelly:"AI will transform society in ways we can't predict, but its ultimate purpose should be to augment and empower human capabilities."

Artificial Intelligence and Continuous Education

Continuous Education: The Role of Artificial Intelligence in Supporting Professional Development and Lifelong Learning Systems

Artificial intelligence plays a crucial part in the promotion of lifelong learning by delivering learning experiences that are individualized, adaptable, and flexible. These experiences are designed to meet the ever-changing requirements of individuals throughout their whole lives. There are some advantages that artificial intelligence provides in the context of ongoing education and professional development:

Paths of Learning That Are Personalized:

AI can analyze an individual's learning history, skills, shortcomings, and career aspirations, allowing for the creation of individualized learning programs. This guarantees that students receive knowledge pertinent to their particular requirements and professional goals and that it is suited to their goals.

Continuous and Real-Time Evaluation and Feedback:

Artificial intelligence-driven platforms can deliver instant feedback on assignments and exams, thereby assisting students in comprehending their progress and identifying areas for improvement. This feedback loop, implemented instantly, supports continuous learning and development. Analysis of the Skill Gap:

AI techniques allow for identifying skill gaps in learners by comparing their competencies with industry standards and job needs, respectively. Because of this, customized learning interventions may be implemented to close these gaps, which in turn improves employability and career advancement.

Adaptable Learning Methods:

Artificial intelligence makes it possible to experience learning in various ways, such as online classes, virtual classrooms, and interactive simulations. These formats simplify maintaining a healthy balance between work, life, and education because they allow learners to pursue education at their own pace and convenience.

Microlearning and artificial intelligence: brief, targeted learning modules that AI adapts for continuous education

In ongoing education, microlearning, defined by brief learning modules focused on a particular topic, is becoming increasingly popular, and artificial intelligence is at the forefront of this movement.

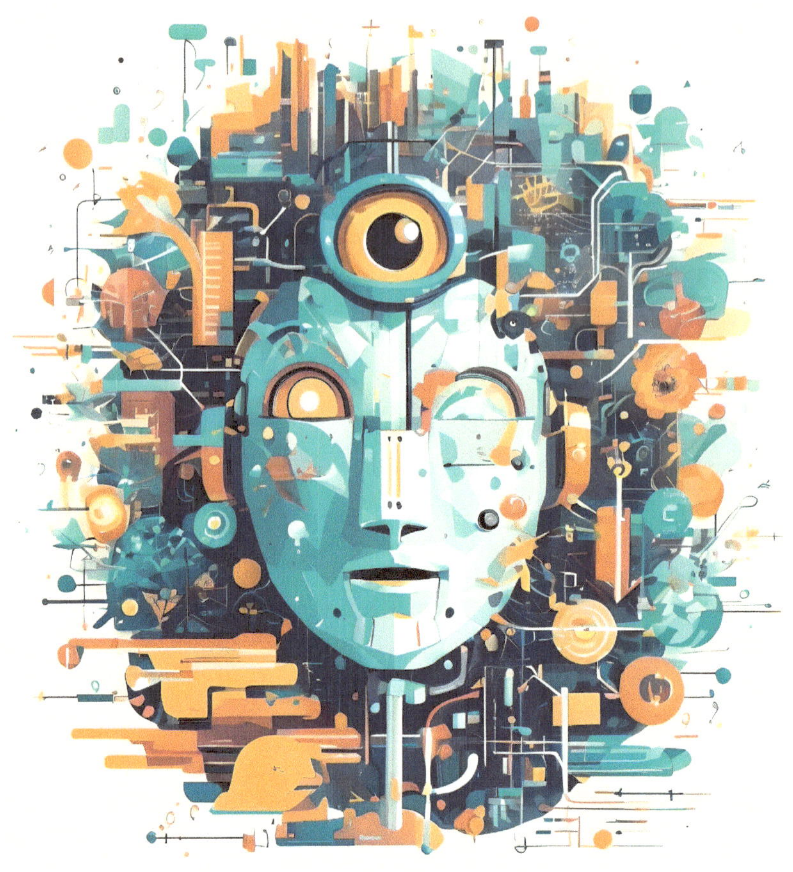

Peter Norvig:"Artificial intelligence is not about man versus machine but rather, man with machine."

By enhancing microlearning in the following ways:

Curation of Content and Recommendations: Information

When a learner's preferences, previous interactions, and performance data are considered, AI algorithms can curate and offer bite-sized learning modules. In this way, learners are guaranteed to obtain the most pertinent and engaging content possible.

Adaptable learning Opportunities:

Platforms for microlearning powered by artificial intelligence can adjust the difficulty level and the order in which modules are presented in real-time. This ensures that students are not overwhelmed by rigid material or bored by straightforward content. The adaptive strategy maximizes both the efficiency of learning and the retention of information.

Intrinsic motivation and engagement:

Artificial intelligence can add gamification components to microlearning courses. These features include quizzes, badges, and leaderboards. These aspects increase learner engagement and motivation, making learning more entertaining and productive.

Learning that is Just-In-Time:

Artificial intelligence (AI) allows us to deliver condensed and pertinent content precisely when learners require it. For example, during their workday, employees can access brief training or troubleshooting tips, which improves their overall performance and productivity.

Artificial intelligence-driven research:

One of the innovations on the horizon is how AI may contribute to educational research and developing new teaching methodologies.

Arthur Samuel:"Machine learning is a field of study that gives computers the ability to learn without being explicitly programmed."

The following are some of how artificial intelligence is transforming educational research and the creation of new teaching methodologies:

The Analysis of Data and Its Insights:

AI can process enormous amounts of education data to recognize patterns, trends, and correlations. Researchers can better understand which instructional strategies are the most effective and why, leading to advances in educational practices supported by evidence.

Analytics that are Predictive:

Predictive analytics powered by artificial intelligence can help identify students at risk early. Instructors can then intervene proactively, offering tailored help to enhance their students' success rates.

Analysis of content that is automated:

Artificial intelligence tools can analyze educational content such as textbooks and curricular materials to evaluate its quality, relevance, and alignment with learning objectives. This change ensures the effectiveness and relevance of teaching materials.

The Simulation and Modeling Process:

The application of artificial intelligence makes it possible to develop complex educational simulations and models. These can be tested in a controlled virtual environment to evaluate novel instructional strategies and learning settings. Because of this, developing and refining innovative instructional tactics is advanced more quickly.

Global collaboration refers to the potential of artificial intelligence to connect teachers and students worldwide for collaborative learning experiences.

Through the facilitation of collaboration between educators and students all over the world, artificial intelligence has the potential to revolutionize education on a worldwide scale:

Educational Communities Conducted Online:

Artificial intelligence has the potential to facilitate the establishment of online learning communities. These communities allow students and teachers from different parts of the world to communicate with one another, exchange information, and work together on projects. They also encourage a global interchange of ideas and points of view.

The process of translating and localizing languages:

Translation technologies powered by artificial intelligence eliminate language barriers. These technologies allow students and teachers to communicate and work together in real time, regardless of their first language. As a result, accessibility and inclusivity are both promoted in global education.

International Schoolrooms:

Using artificial intelligence, it is possible to create global classrooms where students from various backgrounds can participate in cooperative learning activities. Learning is enhanced when children are exposed to various cultures and points of view, which also helps them become better prepared for an increasingly globalized society.

Sharing of Resources and Collaborative Development:

AI platforms have the potential to allow educators worldwide to share resources, lesson plans, and best practices. Collaborative efforts to develop educational content ensure that students worldwide can access high-quality, diversified instructional materials.

Conclusion

The educational landscape is transforming due to the use of artificial intelligence in lifelong learning, microlearning, academic research, and global collaboration. We can develop learning experiences that are more personalized, engaging, and successful by harnessing the capabilities of artificial intelligence. These experiences may be tailored to meet the requirements of learners at any stage of their lives. Through our ongoing efforts to innovate and investigate the potential applications of artificial intelligence in the field of education, we are getting closer to the realization of a future in which excellent education is available to all, thereby promoting a global society that is more knowledgeable and connected.

Oren Etzioni:"The key to artificial intelligence has always been the representation."

CHAPTER TEN

Top 25 AI Tools For Educators

Sebastian Thrun:"AI is about machines that can solve problems, understand language, and perceive the world in the way that humans do."

An expanded list of twenty-five artificial intelligence tools that can be of use to educators in a variety of facets of their teaching practices is as follows:

In Edmodo:

A system that uses artificial intelligence to personalize students' educational experiences by offering materials and assignments based on their preferences and requirements.

Kahoot! :

It utilizes artificial intelligence to develop engaging quizzes and games that keep students interested and provide real-time feedback on how well they comprehend various topics.

The QuillBot:

A writing assistant driven by artificial intelligence assists students in improving their writing abilities by providing synonyms, correcting grammar, and proposing alternative sentences with similar meanings.

Google's Socratic product:

An application driven by artificial intelligence that offers detailed explanations and solutions to homework queries of a wide range of subjects.

Duolingo.com:

A language learning platform powered by artificial intelligence that customizes lessons to users' learning styles and levels of proficiency.

Deck of Pears:

Incorporating artificial intelligence into creating interactive presentations and evaluations enables educators to engage students and evaluate their level of comprehension in real time.

The Cogito:

This tool analyzes students‘ voice patterns when interacting online, offering teachers insights regarding student engagement and comprehension.

Technology of the Century:

It utilizes artificial intelligence to develop individualized learning pathways for students, modify content based on their performance, and offer teachers insights informed by historical data.

Brainscape

A platform is driven by artificial intelligence that allows users to create adaptive flashcards that enhance learning through spaced repetition, assisting students in efficiently retaining material.

Education Through IBM Watson:

This company provides artificial intelligence solutions for educators to enable personalized learning experiences. These tools include data analytics, adaptive learning, and cognitive tutoring.

As for Google Classroom:

Integrates artificial intelligence to improve the efficiency of classroom management by streamlining the process of assigning assignments, evaluating students, and communicating with teachers and students.

The Nearpod:

Creates interactive lessons, quizzes, and virtual reality experiences that engage students and offer teachers real-time feedback. This is accomplished through the use of artificial intelligence.

SMART Learning Suite

A platform supplemented with artificial intelligence that incorporates interactive whiteboards, tools for delivering lessons, and collaborative learning capabilities to increase classroom participation.

Navigate the EAB:

A platform powered by artificial intelligence that helps students succeed by detecting students who are in danger, giving individualized guidance, and facilitating early intervention.

ChatterHigh.

Artificial intelligence provides students with information on college readiness and activities to explore potential careers, assisting them in making well-informed decisions about their future.

Spark from Adobe:

A tool powered by artificial intelligence that allows users to create multimedia presentations, images, and films that boost inventiveness and digital storytelling in educational settings.

The Cognii:

A virtual assistant powered by artificial intelligence that offers automated evaluation and feedback for open-ended questions, thereby encouraging active learning and the development of critical thinking abilities.

Mika:

An artificial intelligence chatbot is supposed to assist instructors with administrative chores such as scheduling, reminders, and communication with kids and adults in the classroom.

Woolcap:

Wooclap is a tool to interact, capture attention, and measure understanding.

Artificial intelligence produces interactive polls, quizzes, and surveys that keep students engaged throughout lectures, allowing teachers to evaluate students' comprehension in real-time.

The NoRedInk:

Build better writers. Engage your students. Boost their skills. Guide them through the writing process. The learning platform is driven by artificial intelligence that assists students in improving their writing and grammatical skills via individualized exercises and adaptable learning routes.

https://www.noredink.com/

A Cram:

A study tool powered by artificial intelligence enables students to create and share flashcards, quizzes, and study guides to better prepare for examinations and reinforce their learning. https://cramstudy.com/ The Best Lecture Notes

You Didn't Take AI-powered lecture notes generated in real-time

The Bibliotechnical:

A digital library platform powered by artificial intelligence offers students access to educational resources, eBooks, and other digital content curated for their reading levels and interests. https://bexarbibliotech.org/

The Storybird:

An artificial intelligence-enhanced platform that allows students to create and share comics, poems, and visual stories, thereby encouraging students' creative thinking and literacy skills.

Become a more effective writer!

Empowering young writers to create unique stories with fantastic illustrations.

Storybird's art-inspired writing helps engage students like never before!

Alta for Knewton:

A platform for adaptive learning powered by artificial intelligence that provides students with individualized courses and exams to assist them in mastering subjects at their speed.

The Minecraft: Education Edition includes:

Incorporates artificial intelligence into developing immersive educational experiences and simulations that encourage students to work together, solve problems, and be creative. Minecraft Education is a version of Minecraft designed for education in a classroom setting. Education allows teachers to offer their students a fun and interactive lesson by playing Minecraft. Students of all ages can learn from this edition. Educators can create their lesson plans using the resources available to them in-game. In addition, multiple lesson plans are already available that cover a variety of subjects like language arts, science, history and culture, computer science, art and design, and math.

These artificial intelligence tools allow educators to improve student engagement in the classroom, tailor learning experiences, and support student success through data-

driven and innovative initiatives. By responsibly incorporating artificial intelligence into their teaching techniques, educators can build learning environments that are more dynamic, inclusive, and successful, thus better-preparing students for future possibilities and challenges.

Elon Musk:"We need to be very careful with artificial intelligence. It's our biggest existential threat."

CHAPTER ELEVEN

About The Author

www.authordheerajmehrotra.com

Dheeraj Mehrotra, MS, MPhil, PhD (Education Management)., a white and a yellow belt in SIX SIGMA, a Certified NLP Business Diploma holder, is an Educational

Innovator, Author, with expertise in Six Sigma In Education, Academic Audits, Neuro-Linguistic Programming (NLP), Total Quality Management In Education, an Experiential Educator, a CBSE Resource towards School Assessment (SQAA), CCE, JIT, Five S, and KAIZEN. He has authored over 100 books on computer science, AI, digital body language, NLP, quality circles, school management, classroom effectiveness, and safety and security. A former Principal at De Indian Public School, New Delhi, (INDIA), NPS International School, Guwahati, and Education Officer at GEMS, Gurgaon, with ample teaching experience of over Three Decades, he is a certified Trainer for Quality Circles/ TQM in Education and QCI Standards for School Accreditation/ School Audits and Management. He has also been honoured with the President of India's National Teacher Award in 2006 and the Best Science Teacher State Award (By the Ministry of Science and Technology, State of UP), Innovation in Education for his inception of Six Sigma In Education by Education Watch, New Delhi and Education World- Best Teacher Award, BOLT Learner Teacher Award by Air India, 'Innovation in Education Award 2016' by Higher Education Forum (HEF), Gujarat Chapter, among others. He has developed over 150 FREE EDUCATIONAL MOBILE Apps for the Google Play Store exclusively for Teachers, Students, and Parents. This work has been recognised by the LIMCA BOOK OF RECORDS and INDIA BOOK OF RECORDS as the only Indian to draw that feast. As a founder and president of the IoT Society of India, he also promotes Technology Globally. Dr Mehrotra is presently engaged as a PRINCIPAL at KUNWARS GLOBAL SCHOOL, Lucknow, India. He has conducted over 2000 workshops globally on "Excellence In Education" integrated with Total Quality Management and Six Sigma, Technology Integration in Education (TIE), Developing towards being ROCKSTAR TEACHERS, including Cyberspace, Cyber Security, Classroom Management, School Leadership & Management, and Innovative teaching within classrooms via Mind Maps,

NLP and Experiential Learning in Academics. He is an active TEDx speaker and can be viewed on the YouTube TEDx channel. As a premium UDEMY Instructor, he has developed over 450 courses and caters to over 8 Lakh students from 180 countries. He can be visited at www.authordheerajmehrotra.com

Books By The Same Author

BOOKS BY THE SAME AUTHOR

www.ingramcontent.com/pod-product-compliance
Ingram Content Group UK Ltd.
Pitfield, Milton Keynes, MK11 3LW, UK
UKHW061027310726
14090UKWH00024B/439

* 9 7 9 8 8 9 4 4 6 7 7 2 6 *